Andrew M Burris

Anna M. Stud

The Kitty Cat
Alphabet Book

Written by Andrea Burris & Anna Schad
Illustrated by Andrea Burris

This book is dedicated to Mom, Anna, David and Stuart who were my inspiration and motivation.   Thanks!

My Special thanks to Barbara for getting me started.

For information or orders contact:
A & D Books, 3708 E. 45th St., Tulsa, OK 74135
Tel: 918-748-4348

Published by:
A & D Books
3708 E. 45th Street
Tulsa, Oklahoma 74135 USA
Tel: 918-748-4348

Prepared by:
Five Corners Press
Plymouth, Vermont 05056
USA

Printed and bound in the United States of America

The Kitty Cat Alphabet Book
ISBN 0-9743294-0-1   US $14.95   CANADA $19.95

A is for Alex and all of his friends.
They live in the alley though it sometimes depends,
on whether the weather's too hot or too cold.
Then they all move inside, or so I am told.

B is for bathing, a horrible fate.
While birds find it fun, it's what kitty cats hate.
All the splishing and splashing
    and scratching and thrashing,
it's almost more than cat owners can take!

C is for Capers who's really conniving.
When you think that he's leaving, he's really arriving.
He's clever and crafty, a bit of a crook.
Can you look at your book and see what he took?

D is for dogs, some large and some small.
They're all so annoying, cats just hate them all.
With their yip-yap bow-wowing and growling so deep,
it's a wonder a kitty can get any sleep!

E is for Ethel, a high-octane cat.
She's fast as a jet plane when chasing a rat.
Since it's really not like her to let one get past her,
I think that the rat had better run faster!

F is for Francis and fishing and food.
Not all food is fishy, but fishy is good.
Francis loves fishing, it's part of his plan.
Wouldn't it be easier if it came from a can?

G is for going, first out and then in.
They stand there pondering on where they've been.
And then they decide once you've closed the door,
that they'd rather be where they were before.

H is for Harry, a most hairy cat.
His fur's always falling both this way and that.
With a trail left behind him, it's not hard to find him.
It's scary to have to clean up after that!

I is for Inky, an inky black kitten
except that each foot has a little white mitten.
Inky thinks painting is icky and sticky.
I really think someone should clean it up quicky!

J is for Jules and all of his friends.
When they're jumping and jiving, the fun never ends.
And as all kitties know, there's nothing so sweet
as jumping and jiving with ferns at your feet!

Kyle has a tail with a definite kink!
His tail is the only one like it I think.
Then you look once again, it's amazing but true.
All of his whiskers are quite kinky too!

L is for Leo who likes to lay low,
Lurking and listening wherever he goes.
But Lucy, his sister, likes leaping and landing.
Up, down and up, she is really outstanding!

M is for Mousing, a fine occupation.
Max is a champion, tenth generation.
But somehow Max thinks that something's not right
as mousies sneak by with their cheese out of sight!

Ned loves his napping, his life is such bliss.
When your name starts with "N" that's the way that it is.
Ned's naps know no limits. Ned's naps never end.
Even Ned doesn't know where naps end or begin.

O is for OW! OW! OW! OW! and OH NO!
In truth, there's no end to the lengths cats will go.
Whether kneading your leg or shredding a chair,
it's too awful to watch, best not to be there!

P is for Percy, a persnickety cat.
He doesn't like this and he doesn't like that.
A real puckerpuss, he loves a good pout.
Just open the door; put the pouty lout out!

Q is for quietly just like a mouse.
That is how Quincy moves all through the house.
His heart starts to quicken, it gives him a chill.
He's quite sure today is the day for his pill!

R is for Ralph who loves racing up trees!
Round, round then up, he thinks it's a breeze.
It amuses him greatly. He sits with a smile
to see what happens when he's been there awhile.

S is for shame on the kitties for stealing.
A side to the cat that some find most revealing!
With timing and teamwork they swing into action.
A great meal can be had with a little distraction!

T is for Tom, not a typical tabby.
Lounging around, he is really quite flabby!
His feet disappear when he sits on his rear,
and he likes to make sure that his food bowl is near.

U is for upset and under the covers,
a true test of even the best of cat lovers.
You rustle a paper or wiggle a toe,
Baxter has had it, those toes have to GO!

V is for Val with a very loud voice.
When he purrs or meows, it's incredible noise!
While some might be vexed by a volume so loud,
for a kitty so small, he is really quite proud!

W is for Wanda and Wendall and Wyatt
who think playing with whiskers is really a riot!
A whisker once whacked might hostility meet,
perhaps they had best beat a hasty retreat!

Xavier and friends have never been shown
just how they should play the xylophone.
So they jump and they prance with a rhythm and beat.
Who knew xylophones could be played with your feet!

Y is for yarn in a basket found.
With a yip and a yell, the yarn's tossed to the ground.
Kittens and colors all tumbled around.
Clearly some of the yarn might never be found!

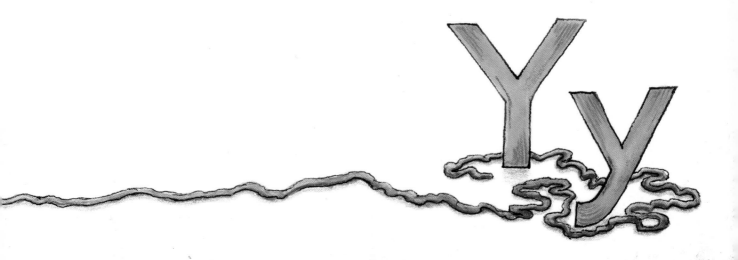

Z is for Zena who thinks zippers are great
On jackets and sweaters; she just cannot wait.
A little bit zany, there's no kitty better.
Can somebody help get her out of this sweater?!